LABS AFIELD

Hunting with America's Favorite Retriever

Photography by Denver Bryan
Text by E. Donnall Thomas Jr.

LABS AFIELD

Hunting with America's Favorite Retriever

———◆———

Ducks Unlimited, Inc.
Memphis, Tennessee
and
Willow Creek Press
Minocqua, Wisconsin

Photography by Denver Bryan
Text by E. Donnall Thomas Jr.

Photographer: Denver Bryan
Author: E. Donnall Thomas Jr.

Editor: Chuck Petrie
Book Design: Dit Rutland
Asst. Book Design: Monte Clair Finch

Published by Ducks Unlimited, Inc.

Julius Wall, President
Gene Henry, Chairman of the Board
Don Young, Executive Vice President

ISBN 1-57223-389-3

Published July 2000

Printed in Canada

Library of Congress Cataloging-in-Publication Data

Bryan, Denver.
    Labs afield: hunting with America's favorite retriever / photography by Denver Bryan;
    text by E. Donnall Thomas Jr.
        p. cm.
    ISBN 1-57223-389-3 (alk. paper)
    1. Labrador retriever 2. Labrador retriever--Pictorial works. I. Thomas, E. Donnall. II.
Title.

SF429.L3 B78 2000
636.752'7'0222--dc21

                                                                00-030833

Author's Dedication

To my parents, who taught me how to love hunting dogs, and why.

Author's Acknowledgments

The author would like to offer five brief expressions of gratitude to parties without whom this book would not have been possible. Thanks to: 1. Chuck Petrie. Good editors don't always become good friends. Chuck did. 2. Ducks Unlimited, for keeping the birds flying. 3. Denver Bryan. Showing people the world as they've never seen it before isn't photojournalism. It's art. 4. My wife, Lori, for patiently tolerating my refusal to grow up. 5. The dogs. Of course.

Photographer's Acknowledgments

This book is the culmination of many years of chasing birds afield alongside countless Labrador retrievers and their devoted caretakers. Most noteworthy among these people are Marc and Eric Pierce of Bozeman, Montana. Their friendship and assistance as well as their tolerance of my cameras in their faces for the past decade are greatly appreciated. Other hunters and their dogs (names italicized) to whom I owe a debt of gratitude include: Jared Brown, Greg Brown, Steve Wilburn and *Champ* of Cajun Outback, Texas; Kern Stevenson; Bridger Pierce and *Madison*; Tom Fritz and the entire crew of the Round Lake Duck Club, Minnesota; Jason Wise and *Teal*; Dave Cocoran and *Mollie*; Heather Andrews and *Sage*; Don Banducci and *Skeet*; Nate Jorgenson and *Nellie*; Joby Sabol and *Moose*; Pat Harlin and *Rex*; Ryan Waterfall and Patrick of Pheasant Acres, South Dakota; Jeff Lawrence and *Montana*; Larry McMurry and *Pepper*; John Bouchert and *Chessie*; Dana Giovannello and *Cooper*; Brad McMurtrey; Peyton Randolph and *Rocket*; and Pete and Tanya Rothing of Diamond R Kennels in Bozeman.

I'd also like to thank my co-publishers, Ducks Unlimited and Willow Creek Press, for their significant contributions to the overall content and quality of this book.

Don Thomas once again did an excellent job with the accompanying text.

Finally, my heartfelt appreciation to an exceptional breed of dog. Each breed has its own strengths and good qualities, but I have no regrets saying that when it comes to all-around personality, intelligence, and versatility in the field, you just can't beat a Lab.

Ducks Unlimited, Inc.

The mission of Ducks Unlimited is to fulfill the annual life cycle needs of North American waterfowl by protecting, enhancing, restoring and managing important wetlands and associated uplands. Since its founding in 1937, DU has raised more than $1.3 billion, which has contributed to the conservation of over 8.9 million acres of prime wildlife habitat in all fifty states, each of the Canadian provinces, and in key areas of Mexico. In the U.S. alone, DU has helped to conserve over 1.6 million acres of waterfowl habitat. Some 900 species of wildlife live and flourish on DU projects, including many threatened and endangered species.

Call to Action

The success of Ducks Unlimited hinges upon each member's personal involvement in the conservation of North America's wetlands and waterfowl. You can help Ducks Unlimited meet its conservation goals by volunteering your time, energy, and resources; by participating in our conservation programs; and by encouraging others to do the same. To learn more about how you can make a difference for the ducks, call 1-800-45-DUCKS.

CONTENTS

FOREWORD

The Labrador retriever has been America's favorite dog for so many years now that it's hard to imagine the breed ever relinquishing its position as tops in the land…and in our hearts. Labs can be seen everywhere these days. Shagging Frisbees with the family in the park. Jogging with the not-so-lonely-anymore long-distance runners that look far less haggard beside these always-vigorous dogs. Power walking or just plain strolling with their owners through urban and suburban neighbor-hoods all across the land. Bursting, exploding with a headlong rush into water—water anywhere and everywhere—the big beaches along the coastlines and larger lakes, the small ponds and puddles, rivers and creeks and rivulets, even a garden hose turned on for another purpose.

No other dog has been covered so much—in magazines, books, on TV and videos—or had its likeness reproduced more often on T-shirts, sweatshirts, polo shirts, pillows, plates, ties, statues, and statuettes. Clearly, we can't get enough of the Labrador retriever.

This fact was driven home to me last year when we published a book called *The Life of a Lab*, which celebrated the lives of, as well as our lives with, the members of this fascinating breed. The book became an instant hit, both with Ducks Unlimited members and with the broader public, selling out its first print run in just a few months.

This book pairs the same award-winning photographer-writer team of Denver Bryan and E. Donnall Thomas Jr.

This time, however, the focus is on Labs doing what they love best: hunting and retrieving waterfowl and upland birds.

Photographed all over Canada and the U.S., hunting a variety of ducks and geese and upland game, the Labs in this book are clearly in their element, doing not only what they were born to do but what they live for. Never before have Labrador retrievers been captured so vividly in full-color photographs, so fully alive and animated with the joy and desire and heart that endear them to dog lovers around the world.

Many of you are hunters and will recognize these as the defining moments in the lives of our favorite retriever. Those of you who don't hunt will nonetheless discover how and why Labs developed all the traits that make them the best-loved dogs of our time: loyalty, intelligence, courage, diligence, a gentle disposition, a desire to please, and an absolute compulsion to retrieve things.

— *D. A. (Don) Young*
Executive Vice President
Ducks Unlimited, Inc.

PREFACE

Anyone can love a Labrador retriever. In fact, it's almost impossible not to, and I doubt I'd buy a used car from anyone capable of resisting a Lab's efforts at affection. But at the risk of offending thousands of Lab enthusiasts who do not hunt, I'll state my opinion for the record: In order to understand Labs truly and honestly, you have to spend time with them in the field. Hunting doesn't just bring out the best in Labs. It makes them complete, and owners who have never watched Labs perform in hunting situations will never be able to appreciate the essential nature of their charges.

Experienced hunters understand all this, whether they work their dogs on waterfowl or upland game. Most came to know the breed because they had a mission they wanted their dogs to accomplish, only to be amazed at the depths of the emotional bonds they developed with their retrievers. No point preaching to the choir.

But to Lab admirers who do not hunt, or perhaps even harbor ambivalent attitudes toward hunting, I would offer a modest challenge: Make an effort to find out what Labs do in the field. Ask a hunting friend to take you along as an observer. Perhaps, under proper circumstances, the invitation may extend to your dog. Keep an open mind. Prepare to be amazed. You may or may not become a hunter, but you will certainly become a more appreciative Lab owner, and you owe that much to the dogs in your life.

For that's what the breed is all about: Labs Afield!

E. Donnall Thomas Jr.
Lewistown, Montana

Waterfowl

Labs and waterfowl form an inseparable combination. Each complements the other and neither reaches its full expression in the human heart alone. They share common habitat in space and time: wetlands and stubble fields, dusk and dawn. Waterfowl define the world the Lab was born and bred to occupy.

Developed as a working companion to the hardy Devon sailors who fished and settled Newfoundland's rugged coast, the Lab comes with water in its genes. The modern Lab's ancestors spent their days plying the frigid waters of the North Atlantic, and only the best swimmers survived to propagate. While it might be difficult to imagine a contemporary family pet thriving under such difficult circumstances, those maritime instincts persist in every Lab. If in doubt, show the dog some water.

Along the way, Labs developed wonderfully dexterous mouths. In the beginning, they fetched lines and buoys for their seagoing masters. Their modern job description may have changed, but their mouths haven't. Strong enough to hang onto anything without letting go but gentle enough to deliver the goods without ruffling a feather, the Labrador retriever's mouth remains a remarkable instrument.

Today's hunting Labs come in a variety of colors, from basic black to chocolate and multiple shades of yellow. While most owners think they know just what a Lab should look like, those opinions turn out to be utterly arbitrary in the field. What matters isn't the color of the coat but the dog's determination. Jet black or honey blonde, Labs will rise in the dark, wait patiently on the blind's floor, crouch beside you while the birds work the decoys, and hit the water like a warm-blooded missile when the shooting is done.

*F*rom sprig to specklebellies to mallards, the working Lab makes no distinctions. Downed birds become packages marked for delivery, and the dog's satisfaction derives from the process rather than the contents. Small or large, Labs always find a way. And at the end of the retrieve the dog will ask nothing other than a brief acknowledgment of its effort.

Labs don't expect tips, even for exceptional performance. Nonetheless, hands laid gently on damp fur and quiet words of appreciation are never out of place in the duck blind.

Experienced waterfowlers all must learn to appreciate the art of waiting, and so must their dogs. No breed waits for the arrival of game with the dignity of the Labrador. Alert, eager, eyes trained skyward...they know there's another retrieve out there somewhere.

All wet Labs smell good, but Labs bathed in saltwater smell magical. While most modern Labs earn their stripes on inland waters, the sea still offers unique opportunities to showcase the breed's determination. Nothing brings out the best in a retriever like the swell of the surf and the pulse of the running tide.

To watch a Lab work at sea is to watch four centuries of canine history play out upon a watery stage. Birds or not, few will ever forget the experience.

Whatever their heroics in challenging circumstances, Labs always manage to be more than hunting machines. While it might not be possible to design a robot to make all those retrieves, it's possible to imagine it. But no technology could replace the essential elements of the Labrador retriever in the field: enthusiasm and companionship.

I've seen even my most dedicated hunting companions grow discouraged after a slow morning in the blind, but never my dogs. They always stand ready to wait a bit longer, to study the sky overhead a little harder. For there are no empty skies according to the Lab's view of the world. There are only skies that require a bit more patience.

In the field, Labs make wonderfully cheap dates. They never care how they get to the Show, as long as they arrive in time to go hunting. They'll travel by boat or four-wheeler; they'll breathe happily down your neck as you set off in the family van. And once they get where they're going, the quality of the accommodations never concerns them. Sure, they love to lord it up in carefully crafted dry-foot wooden blinds. But if the ducks aren't flying in the high-rent district, any convenient muskrat house will do.

Labs are born Swamp Things. Their enthusiasm for mud and muck can provide limitless aggravation around the house, as any veteran of dirty canine footprints on clean carpets knows. But waterfowl thrive in uncouth places: foggy bottoms lined with flooded timber, water choked with fertile scum. And those who love backwaters quickly learn to forgive Labs their indifference to the ways of the prim and proper.

Poodles can swim in swimming pools, but it takes a Lab to mix it up with water moccasins and snapping turtles. They'll chase downed ducks through ooze and goo you wouldn't cross in a boat. But the amazing aspect of the dogs' performance under such circumstances isn't just that they do it.

It's that they love doing it.

Labs view the world as a three-dimensional chess-board. Before the shooting starts, they focus their attention skyward, where they know the ducks will first appear. But once the birds hit the water, they reduce the playing field to lines of rank and file, the essential vectors that make up every retrieve. They'll always find their way out and back, sometimes leaving a written record of their passage.

The important transactions between hunters and dogs take place during the quiet hours, when most of our over-burdened populace lies sleeping. The world turns slowly near the edges of the night, but not slowly enough for those who enjoy the magical moments of sunrise and sunset from the duck blind. You would like the Show to go on and on, like the happiest moments spent with your children. The fact that it can't only reinforces the value of the moment.

At times like this, distance from society at large forges a special intimacy between dog and hunter. After all, it's just the two of you aligned against the splendid loneliness wild places provide. Two members of one team, you wait, shiver, and study the sky. The shot and the retrieve that finally punctuate the quiet of the marsh mean so much more than ducks for the table. This is what you and the dog were meant to do together.

Champions are made rather than born, as every kid who ever ate a bowl of Wheaties knows. While the concept of championship properly belongs to the field-trial circuit, even blue-collar dogs need to practice their craft. Training translates unfocused canine enthusiasm into efficiency. Labs may run and swim better than their handlers, but we think better than they do...at least in theory. Molding their will to our intentions requires patience, understanding, and above all, mastery of novel forms of communication.

The dialog between Lab and handler demands its own unique vocabulary: lines, whistle blasts, and arm signals. Sometimes instruction degenerates into argument, for even the most tractable Labs have stubborn days. But the very next morning, with the very same dog, you may find the mood as relaxed and constructive as a conversation with a best friend.

While ducks on the wing require no elaboration of their natural grace, dead ducks always look best framed by the face of an attentive Labrador retriever. Pintail, mallard, gadwall…a good-looking Lab can compose a compelling portrait with any of them. From a Lab's perspective, the end of one retrieve just means it's time to scan the skies looking for the next.

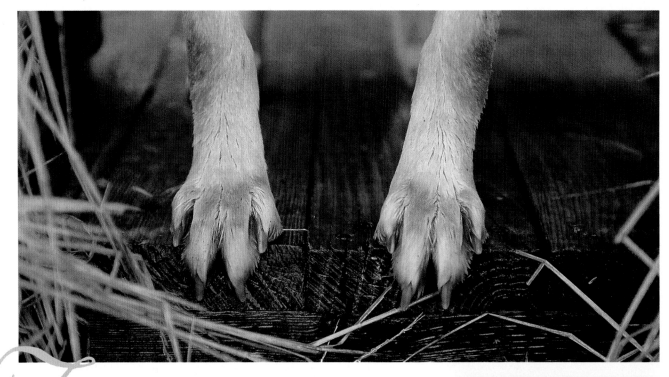

There's a bit of amphibian in every Labrador retriever. Their paws purchase naturally on wet, slippery surfaces, and their coats shed water as if by magic, organizing its flow in tiny rivulets to speed its progress across their willing backs. And if the hunter can't think of a reason to send the Lab into the water, the dog will invent its own excuse: hanging out at your side as you slog through the flooded timber or inventing retrieves when no legitimate opportunity exists.

Versatility defines the Lab's character, and hunting Labs thrive over a wide range of climatic conditions. But at heart, the hunting Lab remains an enthusiast of cold places. How cold is too cold for a Lab? You don't want to be there to find out. In a duck blind, a wet Lab can always outlast a bone-dry hunter. Elaborately constructed of heavy guard hairs and dense underfur, a Lab's coat offers better protection from the elements than anything money can buy… even when it's caked in ice.

The waterfowler's world never remains static. Seasons come and go and so do their participants. In human terms, most of us only get to watch another generation or two join the ranks. But because of the canine life span's accelerated pace, there always seem to be new puppies eager to prove they can run with the big dogs.

While mischief rules the young Lab's life, the breed's best traits appear in every element of play. From the time they leave the whelping box, Lab puppies instinctively begin to fetch. And for those fortunate enough to grow up in hunting families, the world outside the kennel soon becomes a training ground.

Labs don't dither over career choices. Whether they're wrestling with training dummies, raiding the decoy bag, or basking in the reflected glory of a limit retrieved by a seasoned campaigner, Labs always seem to know they're headed to the Show.

The arrival of every new duck dog presages the departure of an old one, and no one who understands Labs can ignore the sadness inherent in these passages. Oddly enough, the dogs themselves seem to have all this worked out better than we do. In the kennel, cession of bragging rights usually seems a painless affair as old warriors retire to the hearth and leave the hijinks to the youngsters.

And rest assured there will be hijinks. With their inevitable surplus of enthusiasm and deficiency in judgment, young Labs arrive in the hunter's life like a walking advertisement for a sense of humor. So batten down the hatches and heed what can be chewed. And if you plan to eat that limit of ducks at the end of the day, hang 'em high.

They've been bred for it and they've been born to its expectation: the pup's first opening day. Recognizing the event's capacity to overwhelm, wise hunters will make allowances when it finally comes time to take the youngster to the Show. Sometimes it's best to downplay the shooting, and even to ignore the spectacle overhead. The day belongs to the dog, after all. The priority should be quality time, not fast limits. There will always be opportunities to shoot more ducks another day.

So take a load off your feet and offer a little shelter against the wind. Chances are the pup will appreciate the effort more than you will know. And if you close your eyes and listen carefully and feel the tempo of the puppy's heart beating against your hand, you may remember the excitement of another first opening day, years ago, when you were just a kid yourself.

Eventually the young Lab will graduate from needing to go to needing to hunt once it's there. No matter how diligently the dog has trained with dummies, or even with live birds under controlled conditions, the first real call to retrieve in the field is bound to produce a certain measure of anxiety, on the part of the hunter if not the dog. Of course, it's nice to begin with a package of manageable size, but fate sometimes deals off the bottom of the deck. Nonetheless, as long as the retrieve poses no threat to the dog's physical safety, there's never any harm in letting the youngster try.

Sure, the first time you watch a half-grown Lab charge off across a frozen stubble field to wrestle a goose that looks larger than the dog itself, you may not witness a polished retrieve, but you'll leave the field knowing why you chose a Lab.

*S*easoned Labs bring one quality to the duck blind that cannot be measured by any field-trial test: the capacity for friendship.

Labs listen when we talk to them, and even when we're talking nonsense, they're usually too polite to notice. In fact, to their endless credit, they seldom complain at all. In the Lab's view, criticism is better left to spouses and teenaged children. But they always make good listeners, a trait that contributes in no small measure to their appeal.

Duck hunting often involves confinement in close quarters, and no breed shares proximity as graciously as the Lab. Waiting patiently in cramped blinds or balanced in narrow-beamed duck boats, Labs seem to occupy less space than most dogs half their size. Except for the rich smell of wet fur, you might not even know they were there.

But like all good friends, they'll always be ready when you need them.

Snow falling on retrievers…there's just no denying the Lab's enthusiasm for cold weather. Of course, that's often when the duck hunting proves best, and after a season or two the dogs seem to know it.

Forecast for the weekend: a cold arctic air mass approaching rapidly from the north…Let's face it: The hard-core waterfowler's idea of great weather would strike most observers as an acquired taste. Thank goodness for Labrador retrievers. It's nice to know someone understands.

And how the frost and ice become them! Imagine the dog's face framed by a corona of rime, each whisker sparkling softly in the morning light. I suspect that's how my own dogs would want me to remember them, for that's the way they always look when we sit beside the creek and shiver while we wait for the birds to arrive.

Despite their all-business approach to so much of what goes on in the duck blind, even the hardest working Labs seldom lose their inherent sense of humor. Don't let all that intensity fool you: All Labs are born clowns. And it's a rare duck hunt that can't benefit from a little comic relief.

Granted, most of us would rather not be distracted by canine antics just as the geese we've conspired against all week finally set their wings. But it's hard to fault the dogs for good spirits. Labs are always looking for ways to contribute, and if they can't find anything constructive to do, they're not above using their imagination. They'll sniff and explore, play with the decoys, and make nests in your gear. But don't blame the dogs…they just want to make sure duck hunting stays fun.

Labs and mallards: America's dog and America's duck. The two go together like salt and pepper. While Labs will retrieve just about anything that flies (and a lot of things that don't, for that matter), they always seem to look best holding greenheads. Mallards fit perfectly inside their mouths, and when a Lab delivers a plump, heavily plumaged drake, it's hard to avoid the impression of a dog fulfilling its destiny.

Labs and mallards even share certain physical analogies. Both look a bit more robust than their counterparts, and they seem to know it. Nature provides each with a marvelously functional protective barrier against the icy waters they frequent: luxurious, buoyant, soft, and inviting to the human touch. Fur and feathers—in this case, a perfect combination.

It's hard to imagine America's wetlands without them.

While wetlands remain central to the pursuit of ducks and geese, the waterfowler's world enjoys broad horizons. Windswept stubble fields may lack charm, but sometimes they're the Show. When flocks of northern mallards start to spiral down into the grain, expect dogs and hunters to take notice. They'll be there at dawn for the same reason Willie Sutton robbed banks: That's where the money is!

Barren fields can be lonely places, especially when they lie still and frozen beneath late-season skies. Cold earth feels harsh and unforgiving beneath the feet, and the wind always seems to bite harder than expected. But when you've picked up the decoys and set off for home with the game strap dragging pleasantly at your shoulder, you won't have any trouble remembering why you came.

Neither will the dog.

Waterfowling owes an immeasurable debt to wild places. Untrammeled habitat produces ducks and shelters them during the course of each season's passage. Large or small, the pieces of wild America we rediscover every time we take to the field offer respite from the hurry that surrounds our daily lives. By doing so they become an end as well as a means, a source of satisfaction every bit as important as the shooting.

Wild places can be lonely places, too, which is why no one appreciates the Lab's personable nature quite like the waterfowler. Far from the madding crowd, spontaneous displays of canine affection feel especially welcome. Emotions shared afield seem amplified, even though hunters aren't necessarily the kind of people who dedicate time to getting in touch with their feelings.

That's why we have Labs around to make it easy.

*L*abs love being wet, and they assume that we do too. Masters of the close-range shake on frigid autumn mornings, they like to treat water as a gift to be shared, and our occasional lack of appreciation usually leaves them looking faintly bewildered. Bottom line: If you and your favorite shotgun can't stand a little pond water, better learn to fetch your own ducks.

And Labs love to lick and nuzzle, just to let you know what a great time they're having. There's nothing quite like a surprise attack from a wet canine nose against an ear to ensure the attention of its recipient. Sloppy? You bet. Aggravating? Sometimes. Essential to the process of putting ducks on the table? Not in the least.

Then why do we remember those moments as pleasantly as the best shots of the day?

The bonds formed between hunters and dogs afield reflect the intensity of their circumstances. Sometimes you must wait to realize their enduring value. Depend on those moments to remind you why you chose Labs.

To paraphrase someone wise, the unexamined hunt is not worth hunting. So take a moment after you've plucked the birds and oiled the guns. Talk it over with a friend.

Despite the camaraderie of the duck blind, waterfowling remains a solitary undertaking. Not surprisingly, duck hunters tend to be solitary people, unaccustomed to intrusions of privacy. But Labs always remain welcome in the inner circle, an enduring tribute to the breed's personality.

Labs don't crowd our personal space. We tell them things we'd never share with anyone, at least not with any degree of comfort. They listen and understand. They never expect excuses.

After the hunt, some dogs belong back in the kennel. Not Labs. Their company proves just as welcome during the quiet times as it was during the excitement of the shooting. Somehow they manage to enrich the experience even after it's supposed to be over. And that may be their real gift. With Labs around, the hunt never really ends.

*N*ext may be the most important adjective in the waterfowler's vocabulary. The next season, the next puppy, the next young hunter…The next trip to the Show.

Kids and Labs share a number of convictions, none more important than the belief that tomorrow will be even more fun than today. As mature adults, we're supposed to know better. That's why we need dogs and youngsters around to remind us there is folly in our wisdom and wisdom in our folly.

The Labrador retriever's genetics have survived a remarkable odyssey, from St. Hubert's hound in Elizabethan England to St. John's dog in Newfoundland, back to England as the Labrador, and back to the New World once again. Along the way, they've become more than masters of their craft. They've become an essential component of the waterfowling experience and a critical ally to the human heart.

Upland Game

chapter two

Although the breed evolved as a water dog, the Labrador retriever never met a game bird it didn't long to hunt. Few hunting dogs have proven themselves as versatile, and today's hunting Lab enjoys a far-ranging job description its ancestors could scarcely imagine. So let us leave the creeks and marshes behind us for a while and see what the Lab can accomplish in upland cover.

The distance between the duck blind and the arid breaks of the Snake River basin cannot be expressed in miles. The journey involves drastic changes in temperature, clothing, and attitude—and above all, crossing contour lines that are often stacked straight up. This is huge, three-dimensional terrain, and hunting it requires investment measured in sweat and blood. In chukar country, triumphs fall not to the hunters with the surest eyes or the dogs with the best noses, but to the teams with the strongest hearts. No wonder Labs flourish here, even though the nearest water lies impossibly far away below the heart of the action.

The essential loneliness of the breaks enforces the bonds of friendship that develop among those who hunt them together. You'll need hunting partners to encourage you to continue up the endless slopes even when your legs insist otherwise. Sometimes those friends hunt on two legs and sometimes on four. Either way, don't leave home without them.

The upland hunter's reward often comes in small packages, in this case courtesy of a diabolical little import that runs up, flies down, and seems to take an extraordinary delight in confounding its pursuers. Appearing and disappearing as rapidly as mirage water on a summer road, chukar on the ground can reduce fit hunters to exhaustion. And when they finally flush and peel away from the hills at angles Euclid never imagined, they can move even experienced wingshots to tears.

But when the dog delivers that hard-won bundle of feathers at last, you'll know you bagged your bird the old-fashioned way. You earned it.

*I*n some ways, Hungarian partridge seem even less likely candidates for the Lab's attention than chukar. Birds of stubble fields and short-grass prairies, Hun coveys flush without encouragement, and downed birds usually fall in open terrain. But once they've broken up into singles and pairs, Huns can hide from anything but a determined canine nose, and their natural camouflage allows fallen birds to vanish in plain sight.

Flush 'em and fetch 'em: a familiar job description for the versatile retriever. While their habitat may seem far removed from the wetlands that built the Lab's reputation, Huns look perfectly at home in the air above a hard-working Lab, and even more so cradled in the dog's mouth when the shooting is done.

In 1881, Judge Owen Denny, then the American consul to Shanghai, sent a crate of ring-necked pheasants to his brother's farm in Oregon's Willamette Valley and changed the character of American upland bird hunting forever. No other event contributed as much to the Labrador's evolution from pure water dog to versatile retriever. Because of their intelligence, running ability, and enthusiasm for heavy cover, pheasants challenged the abilities of traditional pointing breeds developed east of the Mississippi for the pursuit of grouse and quail. The newcomers from China demanded a new kind of bird dog, one capable of playing the running game, willing to tackle ferociously thick cover, and determined enough to chase down wounded pheasants, the toughest retrieving upland bird hunting has to offer.

Guess who that turned out to be?

While useful in the pursuit of imported partridge species like chukar and Huns, the Lab's unique combination of talents proves all but mandatory to the serious pheasant hunter. Wild ringnecks seem to treat their relationship with bird dogs as a personal challenge, and they bring cunning and tenacity to the chase unlike any other upland game bird. Born to run and hide, they'll leave tentative bird dogs staring wistfully at the empty places they've left behind.

Getting pheasants airborne requires the services of a dog that won't take no for an answer. Experienced flushing Labs leave the kennel for the field with an intensity of purpose awesome to behold. Never mind the thorns and the brambles and the sneakiest stratagems old roosters have to offer...nothing deters them in their desire to find and to flush.

In fact, it's hard to avoid the impression that Labs take the challenge personally, too.

How ironic that two imports should meet in our own heartland—one by way of the Atlantic, the other by way of the Pacific—to define the American upland hunting experience. Both the Lab and the ringneck began as strangers in a strange land only to thrive by virtue of enthusiasm for their new environment. Hunting in America will never be the same thanks to this happy accident of fate, a circumstance best appreciated by those fortunate enough to take to the field accompanied by experienced flushing Labs.

So when the roosters are hanging from the game strap at the end of the day and the dogs have returned to the kennel, take a moment to consider how empty the cover—and our lives—would be without both these welcome immigrants.

The ringneck may have solidified the Lab's credentials as our most useful all-around sporting breed, but the dog's accomplishments on the plains hardly disqualified it from service in classical upland bird cover. Decades before pheasants arrived on the scene, American wingshooting traditions evolved in deciduous forest cover courtesy of pointing breeds and ruffed grouse.

It was only a matter of time until Labs crashed the party.

Come October, partridge hunting—real pa'tridge, with only one "r"—reliably offers the observant hunter a visual feast. And somehow, yellow Labs always seem better suited than their darker counterparts to work in ruffed grouse cover: The color of their coats perfectly complements the golden hue of the autumn leaves overhead.

Compared to most western bird habitat, ruffed grouse cover occupies small spaces. The hard-charging Lab may seem out of its element here, with all those tight-knit aspens around to complicate the chase. But the mechanics of the process turn out to be old hat: Use the nose, cover the ground, listen to the whistle. Hunt.

And when the dog has finally found the object of its search, the explosion of wings and the quick sound of the shot that follows become their own reward. Of course it helps if the bird and the column of shot manage to collide somewhere out there in the middle of all that foliage, but that's your problem and not the dog's.

This is tough shooting. Close quarters reduce the event itself to blurs and bangs expressed in little more than seconds. At times like this, all downed birds deserve a bit of celebration. No member of the party will be happier to participate than the dog, eagerly at first, and finally with an attitude of serene reflection.

In the end, it boils down to this: Labs with game to hunt are never out of their element.

Purists may still bridle at the thought of Labs in ruffed grouse cover. Those who can't imagine hearing the roar of grouse wings without a pointing dog beside them are entitled to their opinion. We won't remind them of the way all those downed birds arrived in our hands as if by magic as soon as the shooting was over. And we certainly won't embarrass anyone by asking how their setters would do in icy water on a late-season duck hunt.

No, to each his own. We're all ladies and gentlemen here. And with that we'll retire to the cabin to pluck some birds and scratch some canine ears.

It's all in a day's work for the versatile Lab.

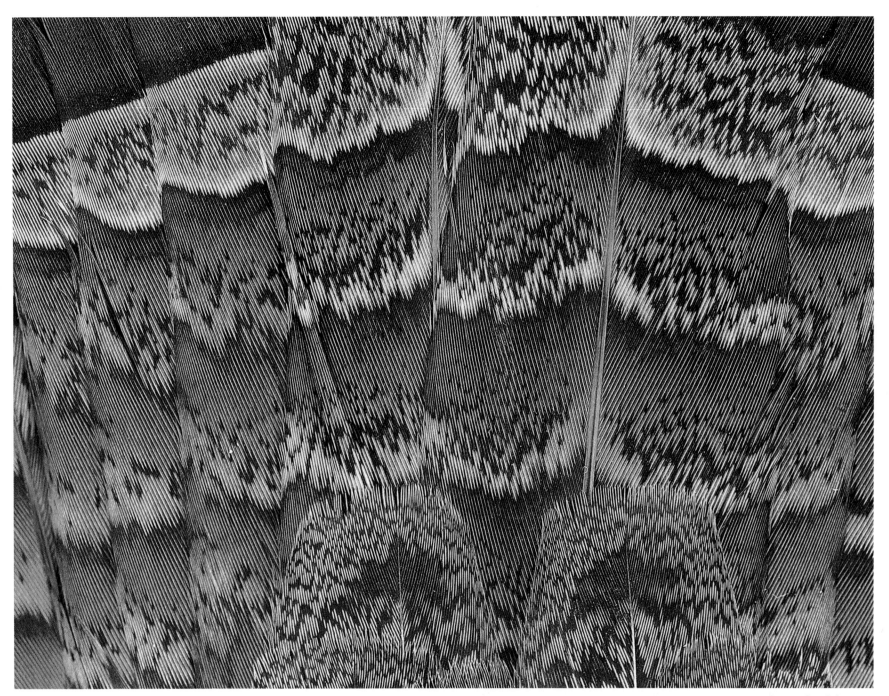

Of course, grouse come in many shapes and sizes, and none proves better suited to the Lab's attention than the western sharptail. Early in the season, enormous blue skies lie sprawled across sharptail country, reminding all who visit of their fundamental insignificance. Large, empty places make good arguments for companions, especially companions that can flush and fetch.

*I*t can be sobering to realize what a small percentage of our time afield actually involves killing birds. Every rise and shot represents the tiny apex of a broad-based temporal pyramid derived from countless hours of preparation, training, and practice. Coming and going. Being there.

And despite the endless enthusiasm they bring to the hunt, Labs often reach their fullest expression during the quiet times. Some might say nothing important happens then.

Lab people know better.

It's easy to appreciate hunting dogs when birds are flying. You can't shoot what doesn't flush and you can't eat what you can't find when it's dead. But the relationship between hunters and dogs should always transcend the tally at the end of the day. Labs always seem to find ways to make the good days last a little longer.

I've always felt that upland Labs look happiest hunting big, open country. Perhaps western prairies appeal to their genetic history as seafarers. They seem to regard distant horizons as a challenge. More cover than any dog could hunt in a day? There's no such thing as far as they're concerned, and if you doubt their confidence, just give them a chance to prove you wrong.

Of course, they'll outrun you ten miles to one. The words *too steep* do not belong in their vocabulary. And they don't need birds to keep them going; the possibility of birds will suffice. But if you're still standing at the end of the day, they'll be standing right beside you. And if you want to hit one more coulee, they'll race you to the cover.

All you have to do is point the way.

While versatility may be the hallmark of the Lab's performance on upland game, I've always imagined a special relationship between Labs and ringnecks. Wild roosters bring out the qualities we love most in our Labs: tenacity, endurance, cunning. In upland cover, pheasants are the Show; the rest is practice.

Perhaps it's nothing more than the noise and visual excitement of a rooster's flush, but I don't think so. Like all determined athletes, Labs love challenges, and no upland species makes game dogs earn their keep quite like pheasants. Wild ringnecks survive predation by raptors, foxes, coyotes, and bobcats on a daily basis. Labs only get to hunt the survivors. No wonder they take it so seriously.

Despite the size of the country the birds inhabit, pheasant hunting ranks among the most social forms of wingshooting. The interaction between hunters, dogs, and game often takes place in the open for all to see. Pheasant hunters get to rejoice in one another's triumphs and share occasional moments of despair. And so do the dogs.

What better way to introduce young hunters to the traditions of the wingshooting life? Even when the birds don't cooperate, vast tracts of cover stand ready to absorb all that youthful energy. Besides, kids and Labs are born soul mates, perpetually convinced that the next bend in the creek will hold roosters even though the last two dozen didn't.

And when everything does go according to those optimistic expectations, the look of satisfaction on a novice hunter's face can compensate for hours of labor through unproductive cover. Accepting one's first pheasant from the

family retriever is less an end than a beginning, and the approval and satisfaction kids experience in the process can sustain them through all kinds of adolescent challenges to come.

Of course, as far as the dog is concerned it's just another retrieve. But Labs are always too polite to tell.

*D*elicate and diminutive, the mourning dove may seem an unlikely quarry for dogs born and bred to the pursuit of big birds in big water. But as we've seen, Labs quickly adapt to the pursuit of almost anything that flies. And besides, in most states doves come first. After a long summer of training dummies and clay birds, who could resist?

So round up the kids and the dog and a box of No. 8s and head for the nearest stubble field. The dog may turn up his nose at that first mouthful of dove feathers, but don't worry. He'll get over it.

Despite the dedication Labs bring to the hunt, intensity in the field may not represent their most compelling quality. Other breeds produce their share of dogs that flush and fetch, but none comes close to rivaling the Labrador retriever's universal popularity, even among upland hunters for whom waterfowl are little more than a sidelight.

Understanding this phenomenon requires consideration of what takes place before and after the shooting. For if there is one thing that matters more to Labrador retrievers than hunting, it's hunters.

The sustained eye contact after the completion of the retrieve, the cold nose pressed upon the weary shoulder, the eager tail beating like a metronome against the air... this is the vocabulary by which the Lab announces its highest ambition in life: to follow you anywhere.

And yes, we do mean anywhere.

The pursuit of western blue grouse has never been an activity for the faint of heart. Thriving at altitudes that would give their eastern cousins nosebleeds, blues depend on contour lines rather than guile to evade pursuit. Successful blue grouse hunts require tough legs, strong lungs, comfortable boots, and dogs that can't imagine an excuse to stop hunting. Sound like anyone we know?

Blue grouse sound like mountain thunder when they flush, and despite their size they're as quick on the wing as any upland bird I know. Hunters who manage to keep their nerves under control and follow through with the shotgun barrel don't want to lose the result of all that effort, for few game birds rival the blue on the table.

So when you start back down the hill at last, headed for the kitchen, don't forget how dinner got from the ground to the game vest.

Black Labs on sun-bleached grass; dark clouds gathering against a bright horizon. Society and solitude. Good dogs always look their best when they're hunting on the other side of the line that separates the everyday world of busyness and bustle from the emptiness beyond. Perhaps that's just where we need them most, not to flush and to fetch but to remind us that we are never really alone, even in the loneliest of places.

Of course, you go for the birds. You go for the birds, to paraphrase Mallory on Everest, because they're there. But after you've found them and taken your share, you'll leave the field feeling less like a victor than a member of a team. You and the dog. It couldn't get any simpler.

Or any better.

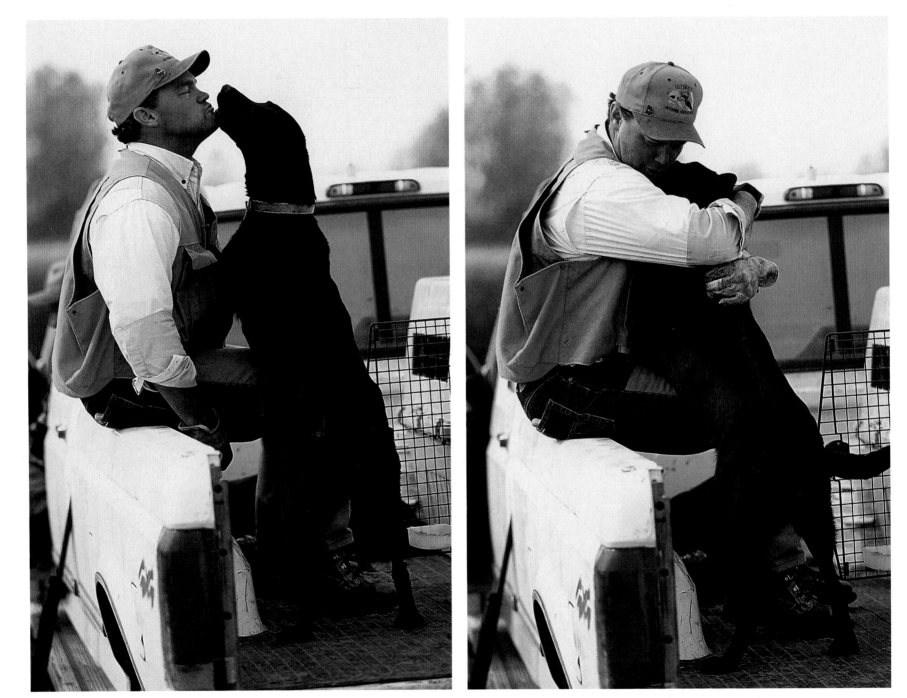

HAVE YOU LOVED YOUR _LAB_ TODAY?

PALMETTO RETRIEVER CLUB, INC.

My personal definition of a memorable bird hunt is one on which I had a great time without shooting any birds. And I do get skunked, even after all these years of experience in the middle of the best hunting in the world. The worst day of hunting, the best day of working…we all know how that old comparison goes. Funny thing is, the dogs feel pretty much the same way. I know because we laugh about it together all the time.

So: Have you loved your Lab today? Let's hope so, because it's a sure bet the dog has loved you, even if you hunted the wrong draw or missed the season's easiest straightaway.

And when all the shooting's done, that may be the best excuse of all for hunting with a Lab.